TRANSNATIONAL BATTLE FIELD

∞

COMMUNE EDITIONS

Red Epic, Joshua Clover
We Are Nothing and So Can You, Jasper Bernes
That Winter the Wolf Came, Juliana Spahr

A Series of Un/Natural/Disasters, Cheena Marie Lo
Still Dirty, David Lau
Maximum Ca'Canny the Sabotage Manuals, Ida Börjel

Blackout, Nanni Balestrini
Transnational Battle Field, ~~Heriberto Yépez~~
Special Subcommittee, Samuel Solomon

Transnational Battle Field

HERIBERTO ~~YÉPEZ~~

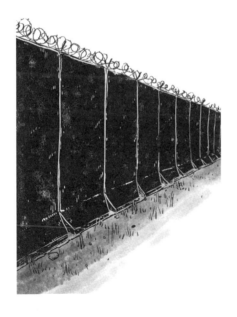

Commune Editions
Oakland, California
communeeditions.com

An imprint of AK Press / AK Press UK
Oakland, California (akpress@akpress.org)
Edinburgh, Scotland (ak@akedin.demon.co.uk)

Commune Editions design by Front Group Design
    (frontgroupdesign.com)
Cover illustration by Amze Emmons

Library of Congress Cataloging-in-Publication Data

~~Yépez, Heriberto~~
    Transnational battlefield / ~~Heriberto Yépez~~
    ISBN 9781934639221 (pbk.: alk. paper)
    Library of Congress Control Number: 2017936131

Printed on acid-free paper by McNaughton & Gunn, Michigan, U.S.A. The
    paper used in this publication meets the minimum requirements of ANSI/
    NISO Z39.48-1992 (R2009)(*Permanence of Paper*).

TABLE OF CONTENTS

2001

I am not experimental
By Will.
        English is not my mother
I cannot be but experimental
Inside Empire.

Nada. Nothing.

Every time you cross the Tijuana (Baja California-Mexico) / San
   Diego (California-US) border — "the world's busiest port of
   entry"—a rite of passage takes place.
"When milestones or boundary signs (e.g. a plow, an animal hide cut
   in thongs, a ditch) are ceremonially placed by a defined group
   on a delimited piece of earth, the group takes possession of it in
   such a way that a stranger who sets foot on it commits a sacrilege
   analogous to a profane person's entrance into a sacred forest or
   temple... The prohibition against entering a given territory is
   therefore intrinsically magico-religious...."[1]
You can legally perform the rite of territorial passage inside a car.
The rite begins with you making a long line.
Estimated wait time before reaching the primary inspection booth can
   vary significantly. It can take from 1 hour and a half to more than 4
   hours, depending on the hour and day of the week. Nobody knows
   exactly how much time will it take, though several radio stations
   give information on waiting time every 15 minutes—but what the

1. Arnold Van Gennep, *The Rites of Passage* (University of Chicago Press, Chicago: 1966, 16).
Also: "For a great many peoples a stranger is sacred, endowed with magico-religious powers,
and supernaturally benevolent or malevolent.... These rites, they maintain, are intended to make
him neutral or benevolent, to remove the special qualities attributed to him.... The actions which
follow an arrival of strangers in large numbers tend to reinforce local social cohesion" (*Rites*,
26-27).

radio says can have nothing in common with real lanes of cars or the nonexistent or massive line of pedestrians trying to legally cross the border.

As you perform your role in the rite of passage inside a car, dogs will sniff it.

Passenger vehicles are not supposed to touch or play with the animals whose job is to locate drugs and bombs.

Dog and agents will walk between lanes of cars and you're supposed to keep talking about usual matters, but try to keep in mind your conversations may be recorded (somehow). Or you may simply be imagining yourself being recorded by them (somehow). Talk about what you want them to listen to.

You should refrain from bringing any fruits, vegetables, live or raw meat in an effort to combat certain diseases or bugs from entering the US food supply. And any weapon, drug (illegal or without prescription), Cuban cigars, and live animals will be confiscated by US Customs.

Once you get to the inspection booth, you will meet your ritual partner—a US Citizenship and Immigration Service officer.

His first communication will be to show you his hand as a stop sign.

He will move slowly, so as to emphasize he's in charge, in control of his and your body.

You should stay ten meters away until he completely finishes inspecting the vehicle and interrogating the passenger ahead of you. When he is finished with her, him, or them, you're next. He will move two of his fingers to let you know it's your turn.

Now is the time to put on your ritual mask. Let your jaw down and remove your sunglasses.

"The metamorphosis usually concludes in a character. Character will not allow any more metamorphosis. Character is clear and is delimited in all its features.... It is a way to save itself from the nonstop flux of metamorphosis.... Through its rigidity, the mask differentiates itself from all other final states of metamorphosis. In relation to the face's ever changing expressive multiplicity, the mask implies exactly the opposite: a perfect rigidity and constancy.... The effect of the mask is mainly outward. It creates a character....

16

Every language which is to you totally alien is an acoustic mask…. 'I am exactly what you are looking at' says the mask 'and everything you are afraid of, remains behind.'"[2]

Once your car stops exactly at the point where he sits in his inspection booth, he will look you in the eyes, which must relax—o your eyes so full of lies.

At that moment, you must show your documents and you must not forget to give straight answers which do not deviate from the very precise question he is asking you.

It is crucial you listen carefully to what the officer asks you and do not forget to answer him directly; short and to the point. Be prepared to show strong ties to your home country with official documentation (only if required). Ties to your home country are the things that bind you to home town, homeland, or current place of residence: job, family, financial prospects that you own or will inherit.

Answer every question truthfully and maintain a positive attitude. Do not forget this ritual is about dis/closure, finding out what the truth is before opening the door of the new world.

He will unequivocally begin the exchange with this ritual question.

—What are you bringing?

You should always say "nothing."

"Nothing" means you're not carrying any fruits, vegetable, drugs, or weapons.

+

A typical dialogue would go like this:

"What are you bringing from Mexico?"

"Nothing."

"What are you bringing from Mexico?"

"Nothing."

"You have to answer 'yes' or 'no.' What are you bringing from Mexico?"

---

2. Translated into English from the Spanish translation of Elias Canetti's *Masa y poder. Obra completa I* (DeBolsillo, Barcelona: 2005, 535-539).

"No."

"Good. Go ahead."[3]

BUT SOMETIMES a typical dialogue does not happen.

You need to remember you must not—at any moment—lose your temper. At this point, don't get involved. You must bear in mind this is routine procedure. Don't lose your cool. Maintain eye contact—though not aggressive. Don't look into his eyes—just open yours. He will enter into you. You should be prepared to let him inside your eyes, clothing, life, wallet, or car.

It's not personal. It has nothing to do with you. Give straight answers. Don't fuck up. Do not try to enter into his eyes. Open yours wide. But not as if you were trying to eat him.

Don't swallow too much saliva. Do not speak in Spanish with other passengers while he is addressing you in English. All of you must remain silent unless your ritual partner asks you again what are you bringing.

Do not cross your arms or legs. Officers are trained in body language.

At the verbal level, remain in the generic. Just repeat what you already know as a right answer. Say "nothing" or "nada" but be prepared to explain why are you using one language or the other.

"How come your English is so good, sir?"

He's trying to know if you have illegally worked in the US but are trying to cross as if you were just one more tourist today.

"Living in Tijuana makes it easier for one to speak English."

"And why is your English so good, sir? Where did you learn it?"

Do not explain that you learned English directly from American bodies. That may get you in trouble. You must not show yourself as someone who usually is around Americans and is familiar with English. If you do so, you may appear as someone who works for them and receives orders and often responds to Americans. Do not

3. Originally published in Luis Humberto Crosthwaite, *Instrucciones para cruzar la frontera* (Joaquín Mortiz, México: 2002, 11) and translated into English by Harry Polkinhorn for *Here's Tijuana*, edited by Fiamma Montezemolo, René Peralta and Heriberto Yépez (Black Dog Publishing, London, 2006).

open that world in the officer's map. Keep your story clean. No
Americans in it. Please follow instructions.

"I learned it in school and watching TV."

Your answer was not the right one. You are not following orders. It
appears you chose to disregard laws and rules of engagement.

You opened the wrong door, Mr. You're telling a story, a personal 1.
The simple question by the officer was: "What are you bringing?"
And you were supposed to say: "Nothing," so why the hell are you
giving away the story of your childhood? It's beside the point. Just
offer generic information. Don't deviate.

"To work with a plan that is preset is one way of avoiding subjectivity…
the fewer decisions made in the course of completing the work
the better. This eliminates the arbitrary, the capricious, and the
subjective as much as possible. That is the reason for using this
method."[4]

Try again. This time don't mess up. Just answer the question truthfully.
And don't forget your ego will just lead you into secondary
inspection. Repeat the preset body of text, don't change your mind
midway through the execution of the piece or you will compromise
the result.

Don't lose sight of the fact that once the idea of this interview is
established in your mind and the final form of the verbal exchange
between you and the officer is trusted, the process is carried out
blindly. There are many side effects that the border-crosser
cannot imagine.

"The process is mechanical and should not be tampered with. It
should run its course."[5]

Do not show any emotions. Do not get caught up in narrative. Follow
the rules. Follow procedure.

—What are you bringing?

—Nothing.

4. Sol Lewitt, "Paragraphs on Conceptual Art", included in *Theories and Documents of Contemporary Art. A Sourcebook of Artist's Writings,* edited by Kristine Stiles and Peter Selz (University of California Press, Berkeley: 1996) 824.

5. Lewitt, "Sentences on Conceptual Art" in *Theories and Documents,* 827.

—Where are you going?

—San Diego.

—What are you doing there?

—Shopping.

—Shopping for what?

—I want to look for new shoes. I need shoes.

You messed up.

—How come your English is so good?

—I don't know.

—You don't know? I need your wallet, sir. And your cell phone too.

You're too romantic. You've come close to the lyrical, even the
   confessional. You lose sight of concepts. Try again. Remain calm
   and uncreative.

—What are you bringing?

—Nada.

—Where are you going?

—San Diego.

—What are you doing there, señor?

—De compras.

—What?

—De compras.

—What? Please answer me in English. You do understand
   English, right?

—Yes.

—So, why are you answering my questions in Spanish? What are you
   hiding?

—Nada. Nothing.

The officer will look into your I's, so full of lies. Between your two
   I I there's a separation—every I is a wall. He will look into your
   documents. He will look into the computer. He will look into your
   I, I, I… He will look for all kinds of information on you. And you
   must remain silent. And your story must remain the same. You must
   have no story at all. Nada. Nothing.

Borders are drawn as rituals of passage that transform you into the
   stranger, the Other. Crossing the Mexico-US border is specifically a
   ritual on you becoming the "alien," alien even to "alien" as your

border name—and requires that you play the character of The-1-That-Has-Remained-The-Same. It involves bullying and a strange attempt to reaffirm national identities and stereotypes—in both directions—a performance of power and a language-game which pushes the alien to conceal and/or disclose the transformation of identity which the borders encompasses. Now you understand, right, sir? Are we on the same track?

—Yes.

—You can go now.

Don't say anything more. Nada. Nothing. Follow previous instructions. Calmly open your hand and take your documents back.

And when Interstate 5 opens, drive without turning back, accept the freeway as a fast symbol of the American experience, how OPEN it is, how the fresh air invades your whole car, and skin, how free you feel. How crossing the border makes you feel "alive."

That's what this rite of passage is all about.

And please smile. Keep a positive attitude. This is just the beginning. Proceed accordingly.

A Ten Step Program
(or a User's Guide)

ON HOW | MEXICANS AND AMERICANS |
CAN KNOW | THEY HAVE | A BODY

1.

(A phone call.)
Receiving a Phone Call
(Long Distance Phone Call.)
A phone call with no bodies
(Just the Long Distance Sound.)
A phone call made on the subject
Of the arrival of the American Body.
A phone call made by the Mexican President
Indicating to Castro
                    (the Cuban Horse)
Indicating to him (Fidel) he has to leave our country (our body), when
    the American Body, The American President (the Son) arrives into
    our land | enters into our flesh. (Castro has to leave.) He has to
    leave his place so another body can take it. He had to leave so the
    other body, the American one (the Son) could enter into our body,
    our sexual body, the political one.

2.

Remembering we have | A Body |

by way of LDS
(Language
Discomfort
Syndrome.)
Remembering
The way the body feels
When the mind
And the voice
Switch
From one language to another.

The way it's going to feel when we
("The Mexicans")
switch into English.
The way our mind and body
                    Become
Disconnected when such a Language Event
Happens
        (to us).

3.

Applying torture.
That's an easy way
to find out
      others do have
(a discourse on) pain.
Applying torture
Or
Declaring war on the body
Of the Other
(The Afghan | The Zapatista)
Destroying another body
That's a good way
To find out
We may have a body too.
A discourse.

4.

Being a woman.
Moving to Juárez.
(Traffic.)
Moving to Juárez.
Being a woman.
Getting a job in a maquiladora
(Ford | Samsung | Matsushita | Qualcomm)
Moving to Juárez.
Getting a job in a maquiladora.
Being a woman.
Getting raped
by a serial killer
or a death squad.
Copy cat. Quote.
(800 women have felt that
in the last 10 years
in Juárez)
Becoming a body.
And then being found
in an empty lot
in the outskirts of the city
with a torn t-shirt
that says:
"California.
The Golden State."

5.

Feeling stressed.
Experiencing our body
Thanks
To the Sickness
The New World Order
Gave us:
        Stress.

6.

Going to Tijuana.
Because Tijuana is
(according to The Simpsons)
The happiest place on Earth.
And it is the maquiladora town
Where 75 percent
Of all television sets
Are produced.
>It is also the most crossed border in the world, and the place where thousands of Americans hang out every weekend, the place where:
a) They have Fun
b) Feel beautiful and loved
and c) In control.

(Mexico is the place where Americans feel they really are "Americans.")

7.

Using
Language exchange rates
(Body Surplus)
Violence is the American Way (A quote)
Violence is the American Way (A quote)
And we cannot help but to be Americans in that sense.

We are all Americans now
(even the French).

8.

Being a man.
Moving to the border.
Finding a pollero.
Waiting for the right moment
to illegally cross.
No helicopters around.
No trucks.
Walking.
Hating the sun.
Being a man.
Moving to the border.
Finding a pollero.
Walking [to what's called the Other Side].
And then, getting beaten
by some American INS Agent
Who needs to feel his body
as the body of a Real Man.

9.

Fearing
Another attack.
That's also
Another step
To remembering
We still have
A body

Left.

10.

(The pleasure.)
(Through the pleasure)
The pleasure of uploading
into the Internet
Uploading
Without our bodies
(The Relief)
The relief of entering
                    Cyberspace
(The Final
            Common Place)
Uploading ourselves
into the Internet
Without our bodies.
Our bodies that hurt so much
And viewing
And buying
With credit cards the image
(just the image)
(of the bodies)
(of the bodies of the others).

Restrictions apply.

A Song from and to the Native Informant

1.

[Music, Maestro!]

Don't you realize? ♪ ♪
You will
become ♪ ♪
a
            cultural
            broker ♪ ♪

    What
    do
    you have? ♪ ♪

What are
you going ♪ ♪

            to offer
            us? ♪ ♪

    A cultural broker ♪ ♪

Loving

        Lobbying

                Sounds ♩ ♩

Beauty is
    what empire
does ♩ ♩

                        A cultural broker!

2. AND NOW STOP THE MUSIC, KIDS

Because I need your attention
and I'm going to tell you
how to keep the Nezahualcoyotl dance-chant down.

I'm sorry to tell you
I may destroy myths
—said the American
Nahuatl
maestro-professor—:
Nezahualcoyotl just means
"hungry coyote"
and nothing else.

But don't
you think
—somebody
replied—
"Nezahualcoyotl"
might have
a spiritual
bent
since it means fasting-coyote?

"Coyote" as a symbol of someone
using spiritual methods
to turn himself
into a higher kind of animal.

No, you need to
remember
the Aztecs
were very much
sardonic

And
"Nezahualcoyotl"
just means
hungry coyote.

I am here
to teach you
Nahuatl grammar
and how not to be
caught
in ideological stuff.

So let's avoid words
that might
fuel
feelings
of
anti
imperial
revolt.

3. THE NATIVE SITS DOWN AND KEEPS LISTENING

Take your place, dear Native Informant
and listen carefully:
GLOBAL
is the new upper class!

So are you
Good Global
or
Bad Global?
That's where everything starts.

These are the criteria:
If you live under global conditions
But don't exhibit aesthetic signs of at least 3 GloCal-
ifornian cultural consumptions
then
You are just national.

In order to be GLOWBAL
You need to consume or work
In two countries
And if you're a migrant
still think about staying
In the least cool one.

"Global" is the new
"UNIVERSAL."

But—as you should remember—
There are some who are more UNIVERSAL
Than others.

Be one of them! BE GLOWBAL!

Hybrid?
Did you say hybrid?
Hungry! You imbecile! *Hungry*, not *hybrid*!
Global is mainly the hungry, not the starlet
Hybrid
Hungry! Hungry! Hungry!
And very angry!

Desertification
Is the main logic
Of global market

Not the all-encompassing
Attractive
Rich, Remixed &
Beautiful, Sexy, Paratactic Gift
Of Hybrid-logics

Global means those who can help my career
Virgin Postmodern subjects of study

And
You are just not savage enough!
You need to get your act together.
Or return
to homeland.

You, Desert Global,
You, just
hungry coyote.

4. I NEED (THEN) AN AMERICAN VOICE (A SONG)

Can somebody
appropriate
me
,
please
?

Kenny!

Can
I
be
yoursssssss? ♪ ♪

Can I be yours? ♪ ♪

Kenny!

Can
I
be
yours? ♪ ♪

    ...BEFORE

           WE

              GO... ♪ ♪

AND FINALLY 5.
A SONG FOR MY MASTER. DISAPPROPRIATION IT'S CALLED ♪ ♪

I want
to give you
all
I have ♪ ♪

In my body
there are feelings
coming out
of colonial times ♪ ♪

I want
to give you
all I have ♪ ♪

To surrender
all the precious
information
I have ♪ ♪

I feel
a pressure
to tell all
the treasures
we have ♪ ♪

I become
happy
when your
face
appreciates
all we have ♪ ♪

Because
you are my lord
you deserve all ♩ ♪

You have better uses
for whatever
we have ♩ ♪

        Dis
        possession
        is in
        my
            heart ♩ ♪

Colonial feelings
          is
            all
              I
                have ♩ ♪

from Ethopoetics

(SOME VARIATIONS)

1.

What kind of poet
Can you make
        OUT
           OF
  The poet
      You were made
           INTO?

2.

WARS I HAVEN'T SEEN

WARS NOW WITHIN ME

3.

Poetry is othering oneself
  & being uttered by another

  is to produce SOCIAL alterity.

  is to PRODUCE POSSIBLE POLIS, i.e., POETRY.

4.

Suppose this poem has as epigraph
Rilke's famous last line (from "Archaic
Torso of Apollo") which says:
"You must change your life."

And suppose this poem
Includes big statements
On life-changing ideas or events
In order to put myself in the same
Line of Western wise men.

And through the cryptoreligious setting aroused
By sound effects and verbal arrangement
The reader sits with us
On this ideological music of the spheres.

And obviously dismisses
The deeper problem
Posed by Rilke's poem.

    Or I could change his verse
And play with it in different ways
Following procedures now
Well established in the experimental
Network.

Or I could go outside
Poetry's time-space
And take therapy
Or have a new career.

But none of these
Would

Seriously respond
To Rilke.

"You must change your life"
Remains
An invitation for
A new science of poetics
To occur, a science
On how writing relates
To particular methodologies
Of life-change
In individuals and groups
Who exchange texts.

5.

Art is part of domination.

Poets personally suffer
The introjection of multiple dominations.
Artists have been historically neurotic.

The end of art is not becoming therapy.

Cure may just be a good subversive departure point
For other kinds of art.

6.

man
is
the
greatest
work
of
art
man
has
not
yet
developed

and probably
"man"
and
"art"
are
the
obstacles
for
the
work
to
be
done

7.

What kind of citizenship
(for example)
does North American
experimental
poetics
produce?

8.

Which human aspects
does
contemporary poetry
     enhance   shield ?

When does c o n c e p t u a l i s m become
retrorationalism
neo-neopositivism
emotionally detached
       cool co-control?

Is AGAINST EXPRESSION
      prorepression?

And what about experimental superego?

9.

War modifies eyes and arms.
Pollock's dripping
                              ////// "dripping," really?
Is also how painting   art ANAESTHETICS
lyricized DROPPING missiles.
exorcized   From Plato to collage.
beautified
                    : TO NOT FEEL   WAR.
How Rothko
g l o r i f i e d
totem light
atom bomb

10.

There's
always
an ethopoetics
involved
in   "writing"
but not
necessarily
always
a   "writer"
aware
of
ethopoetics.

And that's where   WAR

Takes charge of historic performances of bodies.
War
            Our automatic response, yes,
            The structures of war,
            Bestow us, wars, immediate feedback.
            There is one law:
            Recent wars
                        Will produce
                        Future
                        Forms.

11.

The history of Western art and writing
can be performed through the word

c a t h a r s i s

a. catharsis as a purging of emotions
b. catharsis as a translation of conventional emotions into higher
   more ~~complex~~ ???????? emotions

a. is aesthetic
b. is ethopoetic

> a. happens to spectator
> b. — IS SPECTACLE
> c. is carried out by artist ethopoet

a. involves repression, projection, identification
   IS pathopeia — a journey through "passions just as they are"

b. involves pathetics: developing a new
   PATHOS / emotional landscape

> *without fear of the other

12.

THE ANSWER TO THE QUESTION

HOW

      has poetry
          actually
      contributed
      to the transformation of humankind

IS WHAT

      POETRY ACTUALLY IS

13.

Imagining a language
Means imagining a form
Of life
Writes Wittgenstein
Who probably didn't rewrite his life
Enough.

If language games
Only mean
When they make situations
Possible
One question is this:

> What situations are we
> Making possible
> Through our postlanguage
> Games?

14.

When sitting and feeling the wind coming
        Through the trees
        Outside   I think
        What is the relationship
        Between the Poetry Foundation
        & the CIA
            Today?

The CIA shaped
The Writers' Workshops
That shaped you.

Is there a shape
Capable of thinking THIS
Without being a shape shaped
By the CIA?

The wind blows through the trees.
Poetry and the CIA have a history.

15.

[Post]Gulf War Poetics.

American government
, oil

Conceptual poets
, text

How [to] appropriate
E+V+E+R+Y+T+H+I+N+G

16.

If Neruda was assassinated
Through a lethal injection in the stomach

It was the Chilean government.

And if it was the Chilean government
Who assassinated Neruda

It was the North American government.

Pinochet is Another.
Another means CIA.

The Chilean 9-11 coup d'état hit
Neruda's stomach.

The imperial syringe
Poisoned poetry's tissues
from North to South.

And if it was the CIA dictatorship
Who assassinated
The greatest poet of the 20th Century,
What kind of poet were you
de facto made into?

And what kind of poet
must you become in knowing
the CIA dictatorship killed Neruda?

17.

::::::::::::::::::::::::::::::::::::::FORM::
disCONTENT struggles with FORM.
FORM represses social struggles.
FORM is designed to prevent expression
of vulgar popular explosive unwelcomed forces.
FORM will always be on the side of the enemy.
As poets, here we are, on the wrong side.
Poets, look around, you are surrounded
by FORM's defense forces.
Forget about FORM
:::::::::::::::::::::::::::::::::::USE BOMBS:::::::::::::::::::::::::::::::::::::::

18.

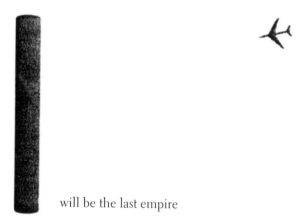

will be the last empire

Poetry in a Time of Crisis

First I would like to say two things:

One, I believe poetry exclusively occurs when it is discussed [i.e. "Poetry" as a privileged structure is an anachronistic notion. I can only stand poetry in the context of prose].

Two, Americans should leave Afghanistan and Iraq so writers and clerks can move to more boring topics.

I've learned something over the years. [I noticed how my English derives from clichés, as if I was writing from the debris; what Eileen Myles said at the conference after telling her story about reading in English in Russia and the reaction of the audience, "Writing with a filthy language."]

"If I've learned something over the years." The instant we're talking about crisis we are hidings ours.

[This comes from my Mexican background and my training in Gestalt psychotherapy; the projections we make; how to recuperate those projections in order to reorganize the self; to not impose them on the world. It also comes from Guangfan's "There is nothing in the whole universe that is not you"; the basic Upanishad teaching "Thou are you" and Hegel's comment at his *Phenomenology of Spirit* regarding philosophy starting only once we recognized ourselves in/ with the absolute other. Mexican popular culture says: "No te hagas pato" (lit. don't make yourself a duck, meaning, don't pretend you are not you, don't turn into a third person in order to not assume the responsibilities of knowing you are the person you accuse, don't become 3 in order to not accept you are both 1 and 2].

I take "crisis" as a crisis I too am provoking. At the same time the victim and the agent of imperialism in every case. Something I share with Americans.

Iraq, for example, is Bush's way to hide he is the crisis itself.

Bush is our way to hide we are Bush.

It's easy to blame governments when they in fact do represent awful societies.

I can only call poetry the most critical voice against every order, including its own.

I suspect as poets we take advantage of times of crisis to try to offer poetry as part of the solution. Maybe to hide poetry as part of the problem.

In saying "Poetry in a time of crisis" I certified poetry.

I certified it as part of a time.

As part of a time of crisis, which is something really good for poetry.

Poetry in a time of crisis must be useful. At least in that phrase.

That phrase is optimistic.

It makes poetry look good.

Part of the solution. Not part of the problem.

But I think poetry is part of the problem.

In a way Bush does poetry too.

I may say his poetry is pretty bad but it's poetry too.

Bush tries to cling to meaning. He tries to make the audience feel the ecstasy of words. He performs.

The president behaves similarly to poets I know.

I am now doing what Bush does much better than me.

No wonder poets decide to be poets. They become Bush.

There's only one step from the blank page to the White House. I'm in it.

I am Bush.

Poetry in a time of crisis can also mean poetry is an emergency measure.

Poetry as something you reuse or return to when things get worst.

For example, if you're depressed. Or there's a war down there in Iraq.

You can make an anthology out of emergency poetry like this.

Poetry is part of the problem.

Emergency measures follow a psychology of panic.

Red or yellow alerts.

Put some poetry into the dying nation, into the dying discourse.

Poetry in a time of crisis. Poetry in yellow alert. Or red.

How can poetry help?

Somebody may offer this clue: poetry can help by not getting in the way. For example promoting the end of speeches. A country where every politician that tries to give a speech — especially a speech to the nation — is killed.

[I liked Walter Lew's approach, "talking again" about Spirit as something you need before doing poetry. And after. No spirit, no poetry. What he meant by "Spirit" I think was the beyond-deep-cultures-are.]

Yet that clue would only be a pretty bad joke.

The way poetry does not help.

It's not part of the solution but just part of the laughter.

Mexico and the United States are nations that resemble each other too much. They should be completely different, so different that they should go to war every two or three months. Instead they go to bed every four years.

Countries that laugh too much. Part of the problem is laughter.

How come you laugh when a political joke is done?

Why SNL?

How did we get to this point?

Because poetry worked.

What poetry aims at, building the common I, the Nosotros, the We / was achieved.

Homer wanted to praise the heroes. He did. The heroes were praised.

Whitman sang America. He achieved his goal.

Poetry is full of successes.

Poetry has been historically linked to war.

Poetry is always trying to put an end to a war that continues wars that poetry helped to instigate.

Whitman is full of bullshit American poetry hasn't gotten rid of.

Whitman was very American. Free verse means having no meters. No limits. Respecting no borders. Free verse breaks the territories, makes it bigger. Free verse was how poetry materialized on the page the imperialism of the United States. Why being American was the best thing that could happen to the rest of the continent.

Free verse explains how Mexico was robbed of half its territory through a takeover, an expansion of the map of the United States.

In fact, Whitman supported that war.

Whitman wanted to construct a space-time where/when everything fit. That's why Whitman broke the conventions of how much text could be written, how long the line could be. That's why Whitman wrote so much. Wrote those heroic lists, those listings. Groceries of History. The many landscapes. The different peoples. Every thing: America.

[I am here trying to start a discussion on how from Whitman to Stein, the way "America" writes reflects/refracts the imperialism this writing is developing under, developing in its own structures. Acker would have agreed on this I think.]

So, from this point on we are going to call "America" the image of a space-time where/when everything is there/then. The containment of All. What Pound called "Vortex" and Borges "Aleph."

What we forget conceiving such a total-time/space is that a system of simultaneous realities taking place at once would make all of them absurd.

"America" is a comical nightmare.

Viewing poetry in a time of crisis doesn't help to put an end to the crisis, it only helps to make poetry (again) a possible solution, a praxis that can really mean something good for the culture it belongs to; viewing poetry in a time of crisis puts the emphasis on the time of crisis, erases the fact that the institution of poetry is part of the crisis, that poetry is in a crisis itself.

[My reading of Efraín Huerta, Nicanor Parra, Renato Leduc, etc. gave me these ideas from the start: we received literary "poetry" from the Western tradition, at one point we dominated that and even contributed our own thing to It, but let's not forget "poetry" is part of the Western colonial heritage, a post-colonial self-critique stance implies a going beyond "poetry."]

Times of crisis help poetry hide its own crisis. I think instead of thinking how poetry can help in a time of crisis, think how poetry has collaborated for the production of a crisis, how that production of a crisis makes a culture risk itself, and thus having to strengthen the strategies to perpetuate itself using the institution of crisis as an excuse.

To make poetry a possible measure. To make ourselves forget we live in cultures that are dying, cultures that want to kill.

I think poetry is part of the obscurity.

I think poetry is the place where people go when they want to miss therapy.

The place people go when they are too snob to go to the movies but they still want to pretend their life can have meaning as their moon, an elevator to acquire more power or at least meet the readers.

The readers, that group of people who want the same stuff poets crave for, but don't have the courage even to write.

Or to corrupt themselves in order to publish.

What I am saying is I don't believe poetry can be fixed.

Nor do I believe poetry should be saved.

(How much more I would have enjoyed 9-11 if the twin towers had been full, completely packed, with poetry books.)

I think Wittgenstein was right when he realized he should concentrate on proving philosophy could do basically nothing.

When crises arise I'm one of those people that think words can help prevent the catastrophe. This is one of the reasons I consider myself a poet. I believe in alerts. I'm part of the problem.

Poetry should not look for ways to survive. But the poet, at least, should make an effort to disclose all the information she or he has historically used to gain authority.

Even a dying cultural practice like poetry can be more honest than usual politics.

Poetry should unveil where its authority comes from. Should push its own contradictions, let them come out of the closet. Should push the crisis further until the authorities that created it to remain in power are removed by the continuation of the crisis, until nothing remains.

I came from all the way from Mexico, stood in a line, asked for a permit, said hi to American Immigration agents, lied in the airport, ate peanuts, had a ride, I came all the way from Mexico to basically accept I have nothing to say.

I only come here to do what I think poets should do every opportunity they have: contradict ourselves all we can right in front of the audience we once tried to convince poetry was something good, something we should share, something that helped. Publicly and very openly contradict ourselves until the laughter stops, until there's no credibility left in the authority we inherit or won ourselves, until it is made clear those who have authority have stolen it.

The function of poetry is to lose its function. The function of poetry is to diminish the general notion of authority.

*Bad Tripping the
White Dream Poem*

June 2015's issue of *Poetry* journal published "Beatitudes Visuales Mexicanas" by Lawrence Ferlinghetti. The piece is a series of journal entries—dated October-November 1975—containing poetic neo-memories about a Mexican journey done by Ferlinghetti. The timing of this publication was a huge bad trip.

This publication shows how out of touch with non-North American communities many North American authors and editors can be even in moments when discussions about race are shaking the trans-national experimental literary field.

As a Tijuana writer both left of the Mexico City literary hegemony and North American experimental circles, I only have two options after reading Ferlinghetti's piece. I can either let it go as one more (one more!) piece by a North American poet telling us how Olsonian he is Down There in Mexico or put in writing why such North American lyrical fantasies are totally anachronistic and unacceptable today both in the South and the North.

In the following electronic performance paper I will first try to show how empire writes beautiful poetry and then I will show how showing empire writes beautiful poetry cannot be accomplished in the form of the sane essay.

At some point during this piece I may abandon common sense and most Reason. Reason is the way empire messes with your mind but not the way we experience empire. Reasonable essays are just as colonial (colonizing) as Eurocentric poetry.

I will begin calling our attention to the date and title of Mr. Ferlinghetti's piece. (Please imagine you are seeing a powerpoint slide every time I quote Ferlinghetti and then imagine me speaking, not reading but speaking after each citation).

First I want to say something about the date:

"October-November 1975"

By publishing this in 2015 under a 1975 date, the piece is conferred a sense of being a "historical" document, the unfolding of a "real testimony," a poetic essentialist ethnography about "Mexico" from the point of view of a North American innovative white poet.

"Beatitudes Visuales Mexicanas" ("Mexican visual beatitudes.")

This is how Ferlinghetti's piece is titled.

"Beatitudes" alludes to this North American poet's insistence on his literary affiliation and his validity today. It also adds a non-secular aura to the work.

Exactly why these are "visual" notes or why they are "Mexican" is not clear at all. The beatitudes part, again, is clear: it is asking the reader to feel these notes come from a saint-poet, a poet familiar to Heaven.

And because North American poets from this period try to resemble Jesus Christ, imagining the Poet as Celestial is easy for most readers. Poets initiate them into the Light [coming from empire]. "La Luz del Mundo," as entry number 1 says:

"Bus to Veracruz via Puebla + Xalapa ... Adobe house by highway, with no roof and one wall, covered with words: la luz del mundo."

And then after reading the first three annotations, you understand you are reading exoticizing literary journal entries by a North American poet-saint-tourist who thinks too highly of his own clichés. But then a "White god" appears at the center of the "Mexican" landscape:

"Halfway to Xalapa a great white volcano snow peak looms up above the hot altiplano — White god haunting Indian dreams."

"White god," ok, Mr. Ferlinghetti, I get you. "White god haunting Indian dreams." Which translated into decolonial English means the White god poet here is dreaming of Indian bodies dreaming of a White god. So the question is why does the North American neoromantic (beat) poet need to dream about that?

If Ferlinghetti was totally aware of what he was writing in 1975 and aware of what he was publishing in 2015, the answer is that he has Eurocentric dreams about the Mexican-other ("Indians"). But my hypothesis is that Ferlinghetti was not completely aware of what he was writing then and is publishing now, as the writing shows: this series of notes are writing themselves and writing (reinscribing) the North American poetic subject as he romantically inferiorizes "Mexico."

Ferlinghetti's piece is the one dreaming of the "White god," and as part of this dream, North American white-writing dreams Ferlinghetti himself. And the "Indians" are just psychopolitical projections of this complex lyrical subject.

(For practical purposes, I will call this military-complex lyrical subject here "Ferlinghetti." But Ferlinghetti is not just Ferlinghetti).

Ferlinghetti is basically writing his Mexican journal (and *Poetry* journal basically is publishing it) under the influence of imperial substances. This is fundamentally a case of imperial possession.

And soon after its beginning, Ferlinghetti's angelic gaze cannot stop itself from falling victim-victimizer of all the clichés from the White Racist Book About the Mexican Dead (including the "burros"):

"A boy and three burros run across a stubble field, away from the white mountain. He holds a stick. There is no other way."

The "White god haunting Indian dreams" here replays itself in the form of a "white mountain," which takes Hegemonic Whiteness from Heaven to Earth, spreading it onto the landscape and immediately telling the boy and the three burros "There is no other way."

But there is another way. There are a lot of other ways, Mr. Ferlinghetti. It's just that you need to question your own authority as a North American white male high saint lyrical subject.

The piece continues: "Deep yellow flowers in the dusk by the road, beds of them stretching away into darkness. A moon the same color comes up."

Notice how by now, his representation of sublime nature has absorbed the White god mythology, and displays itself as a simultaneity of "deep yellow flowers" and a "moon the same color" (coming up). This is a sort of Zen poem used to say the lower and the upper worlds obey the same set of light-colored cosmic laws. This is how empire sings, how it sings while it encroaches itself into nature, and ultimately how one older imperial poetics serves a younger.

By now, of course, most readers will fall into imperial poetic arrest very nicely, because the operation has been seductively carried out and Western civilization simply does not educate its citizens to disengage themselves from imperial poetics. Bodies react and love the Poet's words.

But, Mr. Poet, I know what you are doing. I am a poet too. And I too sing "America" against my will. And now I am inside of your poem, because "America" has swallowed the entire world, and we are not sure if "Mexico" is real anymore, but I was told that in Your Poem my fatherland and my mothertongue are living now. But I don't see them, Mr. Poet, I just see a delusion by a White god.

And you and me are inside this delusion. This is why I am writing in English (and not you writing in Spanish). This is why I came to North American poetics (and not you to Latin American poetics). Because you are in charge and we are tired. Some of us need to come and blow up this white North American delusion.

See that yellow bright in the night sky, Mr. White Poet-god? Well, that's your fucking yellow moon and your fucking White god exploding.

And the prose poem or whateva continues:

"As the bus turns + turns down the winding hill, moon swings wildly from side to side. It has had too many pathetic phalluses written about it to stand still for one more."

But then why are you making us stand still for more North American pathetic phalluses?

Ok, let me guess…. You want us to listen to you telling us all this ecopoetic dogshit because here it comes! Here comes your next grand self-portrait down there in Mexxxi Co.:

"In Xalapa I am a head taller than anyone else in town—A foot of flesh and two languages separate us."

Oh, so you indeed are the White Mountain-god? How great of you, Mr. Ferlinghetti, so handsome and tall, to separate from us, but before you go on with your sweet hegemonic demonic lyrical quickie attack, let's clarify something: it is not a foot of flesh and two languages that separate us, but five centuries of renewable colonial affects and monolingualism.

And by now, we can also see how the White Poet is insisting so much in putting himself in the upper world ("I am a head taller than anyone else in town…"), so thanks to you and your great merciful powers we know we are in the lower level, thank you very much, and now let me continue in the hot altiplano, with my three burro-amigos and the certainty (conferred by The Almighty) that "There is no other way."

But before I start crying under a palm tree and start drinking the coconuts and then the tequila and finally fall asleep wrapped in a tortilla under my big sombrero until the zopilotes eat me during the Day of the Dead, let me quote you once more:

"At a stand in the park at the center of Xalapa I eat white corn on the cob with a stick in the end, sprinkled with salt, butter, grated cheese + hot sauce. The dark stone Indian who hands it to me has been standing there three thousand years."

You really like sticks, right? Don't you think that so many sticks are saying something about the pathetic phalluses? And why are you dreaming that the "small" man raising his hand to try to reach your Highness is a "dark stone Indian"? Why do you need to see non-human dark stones instead of human foreign-inferiorized-brown bodies? And why do you fantasize him as having three thousand years? This is 2015, Mr. White Poet, don't patronize your readers and don't inferiorize and primitivize Mexican bodies. We are really tired of this. D. H. Lawrence already did it a century ago and we don't want to read one more Lawrence Mexplaining us again.

Please remember this has been happening for more than 500 years (do you realize how much your "Mexican" notes resemble Hernán Cortés' letters?; the similarities are revealing, please read that), yes, for 5 fucking hundred years, but none of us has been here for the entire 500 years, each of us has died at 57, 14 and many at 3 or 9, so for you to tell us some of us are a three thousand year old dark stone handing you (Up There) some "white corn" is really insulting today, this kind of poetry is totally exhausted, offensive, absurd, openly imperial (also) today. Maybe some decades ago it was cool, countercultural or something, but now is totally unacceptable.

What? Are you saying I'm mad? Yes, I'm mad, I am angry! And what is your response? What? What are you saying now?

"I'm taking this trip from Mexico City to the Gulf of Mexico and back without any bag or person—only what I can carry in my pockets. The need for baggage is a form of insecurity."

What?

What?

No, this is your mystical arrogance, your total psychic colonial inflation and your colonial baggage saying this. It's because you were a North American upper-hippie poet-editor travelling to Mexico that you were able to do that. The Mexican working class that used buses then and still uses them now do carry baggage because they are not North American upper-hippie poet-editors travelling to Mexico who can enjoy the privilege of bragging only the insecure need baggage.

I hope that by now you and your White Poet Friends understand some of us in the "underworld" are not going to take even one more line of your "Mexican" imperial poetics.

"Two hours in this town and I feel I might live forever (foreign places affect me that way). The tall church tower tolls its antique sign: pray."

Yes, of course, foreign places affect you in "that way." This happens because your body was trained in the US to feel hubris before brown bodies. Souths make you horny. Souths make you Godly.

Souths make you Who You Are.

That is why in your aphorisms or whateva you are reporting feelings of Greatness, Universality, and Eternity and your brain is producing poetic imagery in which your inflated Self is equated to a "tall church tower" that "tolls its antique sign: pray."

Pray?

Do you realize how colonial this is? How incredibly colonial it is to say "Oh this "Mexican" TALL church tower tells us (and especially you Mexican/Indians): pray."

Pray?

"Pray" is not an "antique sign" but the Spanish Christian Colonial sign you are identifying with. The colonizer ideology you as poet have inherited.

One older imperial poetics serving a younger.

The Spanish Empire is one of the specters feeding the North American Empire. And its poets.

"In early morning in the great garden of Xalapa, with its terraces and immense jacaranda trees, pines + palms, there are black birds with cries like bells, and others with hollow wooden voices like gourds knocked together. The great white volcano shimmers far off, unreached by the rising sun."

When you talk about those birds, who are you really talking about? O those birds are all over Colonial Poetics. And some of us know who those birds are.

"The great white volcano...unreached by the rising sun," yeah, whateva, we get it, you, the White god, the white mountain, the white volcano, so great, so high, so unreachable, whateva, Mr., you're just having colonial dreams, co-lo-nial dreams, this is what most North

86

American poetry is about, what most Western Poetry is about, what most Poetry is about, fuck it.

Don't worry. We are almost saying goodbye. We will be in this bus together just a few more minutes. I just need to quote you a couple of times more to show how North American poetry systematically produces colonial golden shit.

"Brown men in white palmetto cowboy hats stand about the fountains in groups of three or four, their voices lost to the hollow-sounding birds. Along a sunlit white stone balustrade, student lovers are studying each other, novios awaiting the day. The sun beats down hot and melts not the mountain."

No, of course not the mountain. No, how could the sun melt the White Mountain? No, of course not, how delirious of us to think The White Mountain is Not Eternal.

"On the bus again to Veracruz, dropping down fast to flat coast. A tropical feeling — suddenly coffee plantation + palms — everything small except the landscape, horses the size of burros, small black avocados, small strong men with machetes each still saying to himself *Me llamo yo*."

"Everything small except the landscape," oh, my White God, I see you have been playing too much with the stick, right? Too much colonial masturbation, man, too much "you are so small, you and everything are small, except Me and the Landscape, everything else is the size of burros and small avocados, even the small strong men with machetes, each still saying — after three thousands years of stone primitive existence — 'Me llamo yo.'"

Me llamo yo? What? My name is I? I'm called me? Why do you need to end your bus "Mexican" ride with a chorus of small strong "Mexican" men with machetes saying this nonsense? Me llamo yo, Me llamo yo, Me llamo yo, what?

Now let me tell you and the *Poetry* journal editors something: the appearance of this piece precisely in June 2015, a few days before the Berkeley Poetry Conference and right in the middle of the crisis of North American experimentalism represents another event of imperial synchronicity.

And it's about imperial nostalgia. The US empire is crumbling and similarly to how Kenneth Goldsmith and Vanessa Place are all about nostalgia for crumbling White Supremacy, we are going to witness all kinds of poetic events from whites and white allies trying to *hold on* to the melting empire.

This is stereotypical nostalgic white-countercultural Americana. This is totally Whitmaniac, totally Poundian, totally Steinian, totally Olsonian, totally Beatnik, totally Conceptualist, totally Il Gruppo, totally poetics still clinging to the imperial.

This is about how North American poetics has historically decided to innovate poetry, to only renovate itself, obeying White Western Supremacist Values.

Some central aspects of the North American lyrical subjects are constructed through conscious and unconscious (d)emotions of Being Larger than Others. Imperial Poetics is the spiritualization of Inequality.

And this myth is directly involved in the formation of the North American lyrical ego and was particularly crucial for the formation of the New American Poets' spirit, that's why both Olson's and the beatniks' travels into Mexico fueled a whole period of North American innovative poetics. Their fantasies about Mexico consisted, on one hand, as a combination of colonizers identifying with elements of the colonized through (Romantic) mythology and, on the other, these same colonizers reiterating their superiority through intercultural poetic imagery.

Ferlinghetti's 1975-2015 vintage "Mexican" postcards are just another version of the imperial poetic gaze dreaming about South of the Border inferior-worlds. And this is the 21st Century and we are still trapped inside this colonial pantopia, this mad imperial hubristic seizure.

This mad imperial hubristic poetic seizure creates an upper gaze that looks down to Southern human and non-human bodies, and it does so in a beautiful lyrical manner. It is precisely through poetry that the imperial gaze is justified, sublimated, aestheticized. Beauty is what Empire Sees, what Empire Feels, what Empire thinks. Beauty is What Empire Senses.

The White Poet-Mountain: The Poet as OverSeer. The Poet of Superiority.

In my book *Empire of Neomemory* I questioned how Charles Olson's imperial imaginary created pantopias, that is, spaces of poetized totalities under colonial control.

And Pantopias are all about retromania, my friend.

Now we have arrived to the end of our travel together. Let's step outside this Greyhound.

What do you see?

No white gods, no white mountains.

Yes, amigo, no white gods, no white mountains. Even this cold empire is melting.

On Imperial Poetics:

BARAKA'S DEFENSE OF OLSON

1.

"…most recently Amiri has lent his support to Il Gruppo, a gathering
of writers initially convened to debunk a recent book claiming that
Charles Olson was an exemplar of US imperialism [some members
of the audience laugh]…and that projective verse was based on a
military paradigm, in that somewhat macabre light [some members of
the audience laugh]…because Amiri actually published "Projective
Verse," meaning that if Olson is a big imperialist perhaps by association
Amiri is a small one [some members of the audience laugh]…in that
macabre light, let us without further due give it up for Amiri Baraka…"
[8:40-9:15]

Ammiel Alcalay's introduction to Amiri Baraka
4th Charles Olson Lecture, Cape Ann Museum, October 19, 2013
https://www.youtube.com/watch?v=O1IhRvHoxcI

2.

I'm the "dude" from Mexico
"whatever his name is"
—as you dismissed me, Baraka
because my poet's theory book
explored how Charles Olson's subjectivity
had strong imperialist components.

You and your audience can laugh
all you want. I'm Mexican.
North Americans, of all colors,
are State-trained to laugh at us.

I have heard that laughter
so many times
I have managed to break
some of its sounds down.

I can now, for instance, hear the pain
and the xenophobia co-giggling
along with the arrogance and self-sufficiency
of finding ridiculous any claim
about the existence of imperialist poets
in the USA.

Hubristic laughter precedes us.
But not history.

When critique hit home
you became counter-insurgent
and welcomed the leukotropic smile.

Anti-imperialistic self-criticism (opt-out).
You too were Charles Olson.

[Some members of the audience laugh]

Laugh all you want (enjoy your teeth).
Dismiss the anti-imperial critic
if that helps with
pretending Charles Olson's specter
is not haunting you.

As if all those verses and paragraphs
where Olson poeticizes imperiality did not exist.

O dear Baraka, you too wanted us to think
poetry's eunoia
erases poetry's servitude.

Poets' beautiful contradictions are engendered
by cruel geopolitics.

First you, Amiri, vowed to destroy
the United States as you knew it,
and then you ended up embracing
the imperial harpoon,
loving some inches of it.

It is phallic violence replying to
love of violence—it trapped you.

Who in this colonial context is not Olson?
Certainly not us.

Baraka loved Olson. Not today, but someday
this little history will say much more.
The wound screaming inside
Likes to threaten others—and unfolds in delight.

Voice is mostly murder.

Vengeance will always turn you into authority.
"Small imperialism," said your xenophobic presenter
in an accurate and macabre description
of your relation to the Larger One.

Unapologetic (historic) love of large things
without mercy, large "SPACE."
How to say no to the ballistic
force? How to refuse being propelled
by the All Mighty Spirit Missile? Tradition
depends on the breath of the Lord.
You—who so beautifully worked on behalf
of the paranoid patriarchal machinery—
how could you not hear
the accompanying bullets?
The projectiles and explosions
participating in the plastic coproduction
of emergent form (then and now)?

How could you not see, hear,
all the typewriters, presses, tape recorders,
fast hands scribbling and ample chests
working in accordance
with the rhythms of the Republic?
Love among warriors, heroic wedding vows
did not let you hear more closely
the inner workings of these subtler bombs.

Where do you stop to breathe, you ask?
Where war scares you
Where war scores you
Where war scars you

That's where you stop breathing, Amiri.

Where the Line breaks. And the USA prevails.

You still were so proud of "America," right?
You can hear the Big Pride
when you clarify the USA:
"it's not a little island like England, you know…"
[Some members of the audience laugh]
"a huge place…"
[12:36-12:39]

And when you (again) publicly deny
the validity of a foreign book on imperial poetics
inside and outside the USA
 "…that dude who wrote that book on Mexico
"whatever his name is
"saying that Olson was imperialist
"he just need to read this passage…
[25:05]

I've read it, Amiri. And don't buy it.
Even though your voice seems to believe
the Man's words.

You were deluding yourself.
Raising ideology high up in arms
and wanting us to celebrate it
as a praiseworthy mirror.

Sometimes, you were so full of it, Baraka.

That's why you got angry at the Mexican
writing that Olson was imperialist.

You, even more than others,
were supposed to understand
we all sing inside imperial structures.

—But you probably remained

so deep in them
or believed they only exist Out There.

You could both sing against them so tremendously
—suffering their attack—
and on the other hand be even incapable
of hearing or repeating
a Mexican name.

Empire distorts the senses.

Empire is pain and rape.

Violence, war, the father of All
(according to that "eternal" source). Co-control.

Love for Empire is the rubbish
that divides
those who should be comrades.
And poetry, that weak
and gripless double-edged sword
we were able to pick up
in this ruined time-space
where aesthetic form
still is an extension of war.

Uncertain Confession

If I access the other side of what is real
I enter into an open field where
My ancestors' bodies
Are piled up burnt
And raped.   Can I enjoy the leukotropic Meadow.
                              Paradise
            White Poets'
        To
      Fly
Only if I

And the metaphysical orchestra plays
What for them are soothing songs
That soon for us turn into screaming.   And we run, run,
                                    run,
                        run,
                  Out of our
            Minds
            Wherein all images spring
From unsettled
            Labor camps.

Birth, and capitalism, and death.   That's all, that's all, that's all.

I'll be killed and you'll be bored.   That's how colonial life works.

                    Tradition is
          Terror   And the voice

Keeps telling me to stay   Away
From the threshold   I am
Not sure whose voice is   Poetry for
Us   Is this uncertainty

The Opening of the (Transnational Battle) Field

1.

Concept plus its other, poetics
Feels
  Like a program
Poets' theory is case-based wish-form
Wish-faulted
    Caged-thinking
    Precarious prophecy
Poetics
Paper Prayer Pamphlet

In a gathering of poets-professors wishing
To exercise poetics-as-prefiguration
I want to point at
    And
     Constellate
The entanglement of revolution and coloniality
(Re)animating
     The opening of the (transnational
Battle) field

2.

William Burroughs, or, as he liked to called himself, el "Hombre Invisible," went to Mexico in the middle of the last century, where he reported a fuller freedom. He wasn't the only North American experimental writer that thought the "American Dream" was located in Mexico. Most famously, Olson and Kerouac had also Mexican episodes in the 50s.

Burroughs attributed the killing of his wife to the influence of an "Ugly Spirit" and described it as a "hateful parasitic occupation... a possession...a definite possessing entity" that he considered closer "to the medieval model than to modern psychological explanations, with their dogmatic insistence that such manifestations must come from within and never, never, never from without."[1]

There is strong evidence one key ingredient in the "Ugly Spirit" was Burroughs' imperial contact with Southern cultures. The cut-up of drugs, Northern experimental machismo, and Mexican urban culture triggered the formation of the "Ugly Spirit," a language-centered psycho-somatic transnational entity.

Now let us see how this ethopoetical process evolved.

Goldsmith Goes Global.

1. "Introduction," *Queer.* New York: Penguin Books, 1987, xix.

Here we have Kenneth Goldsmith enjoying white control of global archives in the age of electronic inequality. The photo was taken in Mexico City in 2013 by Marisol Rodríguez on the occasion of the "Printing Out the Internet" exhibition.

This portrait shows how the "electronic revolution" (to use Burroughs' viral words) helped this ethopoetic subject to avoid the formation of the "Ugly Spirit." Goldsmith has co-created here (but not at Brown University) a scene where the hubristic macho xenophobic asymmetrical intercultural dominator self-expresses in cooler ways.

Goldsmith's pleasant day at the remediated beach was made possible by NAFTA, nonexistent at the time of Burroughs' transnational crisis. Another element that eased Goldsmith's status is the solidification of the "Colonial Library," defined by the Bolivian poet-professor Silvia Rivera Cusicanqui as the "colonial appropriation" and management of centralized collections of Latin American primary and secondary sources by North American universities.

Rivera Cusicanqui describes her experience at the "Colonial Library" as a series of "intense and contradictory emotions" running from "amazement to despair" and simultaneous "feelings of expansion of the intellectual horizon" and a "deep sense of frustration."[2]

In order to talk about the "Colonial Library," Rivera Cusicanqui says she needs both to reflect and feel. I return, then, to my point of departure: a poetics which is only concept reduces itself to rational, instrumental "Enlightenment." Poetics should at least be CONCEPT plus its OTHER, and that is why I will further exit the "paper"-form for the remaining space-time available.

2. "La biblioteca colonial." *Hambre de huelga*. México: La mirada salvaje, 2014.

3.

The Oneiro-NAFTA region desires
An active transnational writing
But this libidinal surge does not intend to abandon
Monolingualism. It wants new markets, new archives
To solve domestic crises. Appropriating and subsuming others—
It's still an expansionist-colonial desire. It's Empire

(Mostly) white cultural elites ping-pong Capital Aesthetics
Across the colonial axis. "Cosmopolitan" Eurocentric inertia
Is transnationalism's undercurrent. Another somatic
Transnationalism comes from working class migrants
Using more than one language and remaking culture
outside law, "peace," and citizenship. The inventive
is coming from these peoples

Fights between transnationalisms will define
Tomorrow's poetries of risk. The question is not
To be or not to be transnational but in which way?

Today neoliberalism has refurbished
Experimentalism into varieties of resilient job experience
Neoliberal poetics doesn't mean writers are sinners
It means they are embedded

Goldsmith's old concept reframed
Reaffirmed colonial structures at the other side
Of Bill Clinton's border fence. Goldsmith's appropriation
Of experimentalism strengthened official verse culture's apolitical
    predisposition
Upperclass aesthetic elegance and neutralization of leftist poetics
Northern conceptualism proved to be counter-insurgent in the
    South–Also

Before and after the conceptual implosion
Previous Latin American conceptualisms here and there
Have been coopted, put at the service of the Master-
Slave blood bank supply
Where the conceptual slave enters the stage
When the conceptual master grows weak

Transnationalizing experimentalism does
Not necessarily produce innovation
Although the geopolitical gaze does endanger the spell

Unexpectedly for the now dead Buddhist and anarchist spirit
À la John Cage, neoliberal experimentalism
May precisely be the driving force of its transnationalization
Across the Americas today

If setting patterns of aesthetic dissent
Is one ingredient in the contradiction which is poetics
We can try preventing the transnational from turning
Into the most appealing ideology only if we remember
The transnational is also a non-human agency and will
Trump us

I read Marx's diagnosis of a "world-literature" along these lines
Including his own Eurocentric-biopolitical pilot-plan

If transnational poetics takes decolonial forms
We might co-ignite change. As of now "experimentalism"
Aestheticizes the leukotropic
What tends toward "whiteness," the so-called fine, rational, beautiful, cool
Eunoian, harmonic, and superior
And marginalizes the melantropic, the dark, disorderly, Cassiopeian
Dangerous, deficient, vulgar, and inferior

Experimentalism chained itself to the leukotropic rules of D*E*S*I*G*N

North American experimentalism mostly lives
In denial on how its nation-centered procedures
Have much to do with xenophobia, the job market and imperialism
But as it encounters other innovative networks
And traditions in the DysGlobal South
Experimentalism will lose its national patriarchal and matriarchal
Bodyguards and linear avant-garde master narrative
Coming out of these struggles enriched by a state
Of partial memory loss, archive fever, inappropriate
Behavior, mistranslation, force displacement, and acute fragmentation

The transnational could become the ultimate paratactic rearrangement
Disabling poets to shape and reproduce themselves
Through national entitlements
Never ecological in relation to a larger geopoetics

To separate experimentalism from national leukotropisms
Is historically impossible. The (Neo)Avant-Garde
And the Colonial Library are intertwined

Only if experimentalism expands leukotropically can it survive

Once post-national and post-experimental
Take charge of new-writer's bodies
"Experimentalism" will not be the driving force of innovative poetics

Currently, in ceasing to be an influential network, Language
Poetry begins to fully operate as a tradition
A militant participant in curated history
A collective and disjointed body able to be reanimated
And mobilized by other agents in other times and sites

Today we imagine the transnational as spreading

Through synchronic networks
But the transnational also involves diachronic engagements
With foreign lineages and discontinuous periods
Disruption thus may occur through tradition-work

We can't say the revolution will be networked
But we can be sure it will be fueled by archives

Traditions in a transnational field of writing will not necessarily work
As they do in national literatures, where they preserve legacies
And erase alterities. At the transnational level, alien traditions may play
A destructive role against other sets of masters

Against intentions of non-expressiveness, Language
And Post-Language white poetics will become problematic
"Demons" for others
                              Like Stein or Pound
These demonic voices will probably creep
Into cultures that do not hate speech
Or deal with foreign colonial specters

The transnational is all about demonology

This revolutionary agency will increase
In the case of powerful melantropic, underground, peripheral
Indigenous, Black, mongrel, Non-Western traditions
And networks only if they are radically decolonial

In sum, transnational conditions already shape our writing
And the lack of a transnational consciousness
Allows Marx and Whitman's
Olson and Goldsmith's ultramodernistic
Expansionist projects to crystallize
Our growing transnational desires
Into the form of an irresistible COLONIAL REVOLUTIONARY seduction

All our poetic-epistemic desires occur inside the Colonial Library

The transnational of the now-future
Is being propelled and accelerated
Through this COLONIAL REVOLUTIONARY program

But some Souths desire to unrest the transnational

And force the "experiment"
To become a program of world revolution
Without world coloniality

About Me: In English

I am possessed by the most powerful
Revolutionary force in the world today:
The Anti-American spirit.

But I am written and I write in English
I too sing America's shit.

I am inhabited by imperial feelings
Which arise in my mind as images
Of pre-industrial rivers
Or take some technocratic screen-form.

My hopes are these wounds
Are also weapons. But they may be undead
Scholarly jargon.

I am colonized. I dream of decolonizing
Myself and others. The images of the dream
Do not match up. I am the body
And the archive.

A bomb is ticking in my old soul.
And the life of the bomb

Trembles in the hands of my new voice.

I am a professor in the Third World.
What do I know? Libraries in the North
Do not open their doors. I laugh at myself
Imagining what the newer books state.

Writing is counter
-insurgent. But the counter
-insurgency
    Leaders want our body
Believing writing is freedom.

This is as far as my English goes.

ACKNOWLEDGEMENTS

Lawrence Ferlinghetti's "Beatitudes Visuales Mexicanas" first appeared in *Poetry* magazine in June 2015. Reprinted by permission of Sterling Lord Literistic, Inc.

"2001" was first read at the The Double Happiness Performance Space, New York, November 2001. "Nada. Nothing" was written and read at the New Writing Series (University of California, San Diego) 2011. "A Ten Step Program..." was written for a reading at PS1-MOMA in New York in 2002 and first published in *Crayon* in 2003. "A Song to and from the Native Informant" and "Ethopoetics" were first read at The Poetry Project, New York, in 2011. "A Song..." was first published in *Tripwire* in 2016. "Poetry in a Time of Crisis" was read at "Is Poetry Enough? Poetry in a Time of Crisis" event in University of California, Santa Cruz, 2004 and first printed in *Viz. Inter-arts. Event. A Trans-Genre Anthology*, 2007. "Bad Tripping the White Dream Poem," "On Imperial Poetics," "Uncertain Confession," and "About Me: in English" were first published on-line in borderdestroyer.com in 2015. "The Opening of the (Transnational Battle) Field" was written for "Poetics: (The Next) 25 Years Conference" (University at Buffalo) in 2016.